WIND AND WATER ENERGY

Copyright © 1983, Raintree Publishers Inc.

All rights reserved. No part of this book may be reproduced or utilized in any form or by any means, electronic or mechanical, including photocopying, recording, or by any information storage and retrieval system, without permission in writing from the Publisher. Inquiries should be addressed to Raintree Publishers Inc., 205 West Highland Avenue, Milwaukee, Wisconsin 53203.

Library of Congress Number: 82-9804

1 2 3 4 5 6 7 8 9 0 85 84 83

Library of Congress Cataloging in Publication Data
Payne, Sherry Neuwirth.
   Wind and water energy.

   (A Look inside)
   Includes index.
   SUMMARY: Discusses advantages and problems in using second-hand solar energy in the form of wind and water power produced by windmills, hydro-electric plants, and geothermal reservoirs.
   1. Wind power — Juvenile literature. 2. Water-power — Juvenile literature. [1. Wind power. 2. Water power. 3. Power resources] I. Title. II. Series.
TJ825.P35   1982   333.91'4   82-9804
ISBN 0-8172-1418-6   AACR2

WIND AND WATER ENERGY

By Sherry Neuwirth Payne

CONTENTS

SECONDHAND SOLAR ENERGY	5
WIND AND WATER POWER IN HISTORY	11
HOW DO WIND AND WATER POWER WORK?	21
PRESENT AND FUTURE	33
SOLUTIONS AND PROBLEMS	39
MAKE YOUR OWN WATER WHEEL	44
GLOSSARY	46
INDEX	47

RAINTREE PUBLISHERS
Milwaukee • Toronto • Mexico City • London

SECONDHAND SOLAR ENERGY

Have you ever seen the wind reach down from the sky and grab a kite? The power of the wind makes the kite climb, sway, and pull farther away.

Sometimes the wind is too gentle even to fly a kite. Other times the wind can blow with fury and tear a kite to pieces.

Wind is caused by the uneven heating of the air by the sun. Without the sun, there would be no wind. Wind is secondhand solar energy.

The sun heats the air, land and water at different rates. On a warm day in spring, the air is warm and pleasant. The ground is beginning to warm. A lake is still cool. It takes much longer to warm up.

The air above the land heats up quickly and expands and rises. The cooler air from above the lake flows in to take its place. The wind is blowing from the lake across the land.

There are two different kinds of water power. One kind uses the force of rushing water like you feel against your legs. The other kind uses the heat in the water.

As water flows downhill or moves in waves, tides, or currents, it releases energy. This energy can be used. The energy from the water in a river can turn a water wheel. The water wheel can turn a saw to cut lumber.

The energy from water can also turn generators to make electricity. Electricity made from water pressure is called hydroelectric power. "Hydro-" is a prefix meaning water.

Water heated by the sun or by the hot rocks in the center of the earth can be used to make power. Water is hiding under the ground. Water which comes from deep in the ground, where rock

is hot, produces geysers and hot springs.

Geysers and hot springs are forms of geothermal energy. The word "geothermal" comes from two Greek words. "Geo-" means earth. "Thermal" means heat. This water warmed by the heat in the earth can be sent through pipes to heat homes. Hot steam from inside the earth can be sent through machines to make electricity.

The word "geyser" comes from the Icelandic word "geysir" which means gusher. Iceland has many geysers. More than 700 hot springs and geysers are found in 250 different places in Iceland.

Geysers generally occur in regions of cracked and folded rocks. They usually are found in

This commerical geothermal power plant produces electricity for about 1,000,000 houses.

areas of recent volcanic activity. In addition to the Icelandic geysers, geysers can be found in New Zealand, Italy, Russia, Japan, and in the United States in Yellowstone National Park, Wyoming.

Old Faithful is the best known of the American geysers. Tourists visiting Yellowstone National Park don't leave before seeing Old Faithful erupt with steaming water that shoots 35 to 45 meters (115 to 150 ft) into the air. In the past, Old Faithful erupted on a regular schedule. Now it erupts once every 30 to 90 minutes.

Fumaroles are found in only a few places in the world. A fumarole is a hole that goes deep down inside the earth into a volcanic region. Gases and steam heated to very high temperatures come shooting out. Fumaroles are similar to the hissing vapor that escapes at the edge of a lid when water boils on the stove. This dry steam can be used directly to power turbines and other machinery.

The Geysers is the world's largest steam field. It is located in California.

Hot springs are quietly steaming pools. They do not shoot their water into the air because of the way the cracks under the ground are laid out. The heated water is allowed to escape before pressure is built up. Sometimes hot springs bubble into lakes. In the United States, Hot Springs, Arkansas, is the best known of the hot springs. It is a national park.

Just like the Native Americans who discovered the Springs, people come from great distances to bathe in and drink the water. As hot springs bubble from the ground, minerals from deep in the earth are brought to the surface. Many people believe these minerals give relief to people who suffer from painful diseases like arthritis and rheumatism.

This is the Beehive Geyser in Yellowstone National Park.

WIND AND WATER POWER IN HISTORY

A cavewoman riding a log across a lake held up a piece of fur to make a sail. The wind pushed against the sail and the cavewoman moved swiftly along.

We don't know this happened for sure, but it is possible. Wind power is not a new idea.

Vikings in early sailing ships explored the world. Wind was harnessed to turn the blades of windmills in Persia 2,000 years ago.

The early settlers of Holland built hills of dirt so that their houses would not get washed away by the sea. Some of these mounds were several acres across. But the people wanted more land for their animals to feed on. So, these ambitious settlers built dikes, or walls, between the land they wanted to use and the sea.

However, the land was lower than the sea. Water leaked in through the dikes, and storms brought rain and rushing seawater in to flood the land. The people needed pumps to push the water back to the sea.

The famous Bayeux Tapestry was made in France in about A.D. 1100. It shows many scenes from life in that time. The tapestry is about 51 centimeters (20 in) wide and 70 meters (230 ft) long. In the section shown here are early sailing ships with the wind in their sails.

11

The pictures on pages 12 and 13 show three kinds of windmills.

The Bettmann Archive

In the 13th century, the Dutch started using windmills to pump water. The wind pushed against the huge canvas sails and moved them around and around. The turning sails were connected to a shaft which moved a pump up and down. Since wind is strong where the sea meets the land, the Dutch windmills kept turning and pumping. Even today, modern pumps and a few old windmills work constantly to pump water that seeps into their land.

More than a million windmills were used by farmers in the United States in the 1920s. Then the Rural Electrification Administration criss crossed the countryside with electrical lines in the 1930s. More than enough cheap electricity was available. Farmers let their windmills fall apart because they didn't need them anymore.

In World War II, the oil needed to turn the machines to make electricity was in short supply. Lots of oil was needed to fill Army tanks and fighting planes. People thought about wind power again.

In the 1930s, Palmer Putnam had decided that his electricity bills were too high. He studied different ways of getting electricity. He decided the windmill was the best way.

Putnam convinced several engineers and builders that windmills could provide low-cost electricity. These people decided that since oil was so scarce because of the war, they would build a huge windmill in Vermont to see if it would work. The biggest wind machine in history, called a Smith-Putnam

13

The pictures on these two pages show the movement of the tide. In the picture above, the tide is in, and boats are floating.

Wind Turbine, was built in 1941 over Grandpa's Knob, a mountain in Vermont. Its two blades stretched 53 meters (175 ft). That's about as long as 12 cars parked in a row. This wind giant provided enough energy to power about 200 modern homes. It stopped providing energy when a blade tore loose because of a small design problem. But, by then, the war was over and oil was plentiful again, so it was never fixed.

Water power is always surging in the seas. Twice a day the ocean is tugged by the moon. The whole ocean is moved by the tide, as this movement is called. The tide is said to be out when the moon pulls the water away from the shore. The water is responding to the tug of the moon. The water seems to crawl

In this picture, the tide is out. The boats are in the same position as they are on page 14, but they are resting on the sand.

back into the sea, leaving behind bigger beaches and uncovering rock formations and caves. The tide is "in" when the moon pulls the water toward the shore. The inrushing tide surges over the land, burying the beaches and rocks.

Unwitting sailors were swept away to sea with the outgoing tide, never to be seen again. Experienced captains of fishing boats rode the tides out to sea each morning. Each evening, they floated back on the incoming tide with their day's catch.

Modern fishermen set their nets at low tide. The fish are caught in the nets when the tide comes in. Then, when the water goes back to sea, the fishermen drive their trucks out to collect the day's fish.

This map shows the path of the Gulf Stream flowing east across the Atlantic Ocean. Benjamin Franklin (inset) studied the Gulf Stream, and he made a chart of this "river in the sea."

Another form of water movement is called a current. Ponce de Leon felt it in the year 1513, but he didn't know what it was. One day he noticed that, although he should have been sailing south with a good following breeze, his ship was moving north!

One of the first people to study the ocean current was Benjamin Franklin. Benjamin Franklin was at one time the Postmaster General of the United States. He knew that American ships going to England carried the mail in about two weeks less than a ship returning from England.

Franklin talked to his cousin, a whaling captain, about it. The captain told Ben that American captains heading for Europe were taking advantage of a current running eastward across the North Atlantic at three miles per hour. On their way home, seamen were piloting vessels to avoid this mighty eastward-flowing current.

This gave Franklin an idea. He figured that the "Gulf Stream" as he named it, was fed by warm water from tropical seas. The simplest way to map it was by taking the temperature of the ocean. When the water got warmer, the sailors would know they were in the stream.

Franklin gave thermometers to the captains of ships. When the temperature of the sea went up, the captains marked their ship's location on a map.

Using this information, Franklin had a chart drawn of the great river in the sea, the Gulf Stream. Even today, smart skippers in the Newport to Bermuda races carry thermometers with them.

For centuries, water that rushed downstream was used to turn wheels that ground grain. Water power has been used to generate electricity for 100 years.

The first dam built for a water-powered plant to generate electricity was in Appleton, Wisconsin, in 1882. As dam builders, Americans are busy beavers. Niagara Falls is located on the border between New York and the Canadian province of Ontario. It is the greatest single natural source of water power in North America. The water power generated supplies homes and industries throughout New York, Pennsylvania, and Ontario.

The Tennessee Valley Authority, or TVA as it is called, is a series of 40 dams that operate as a single system. It covers 106,000 square kilometers (40,900 sq. mi). That is almost as big as the whole country of England. It includes parts of Tennessee, Kentucky, Virginia, North Carolina, Georgia, Alabama, and Mississippi. The power from the TVA system reaches homes, farms, stores, mines, and factories over an area of about 207,000 square kilometers (80,000 sq. mi). These users of TVA water power pay about one-half as much for electricity as the average consumer in the United States.

The Hoover Dam is one of the highest in the world. It is located in the Black Canyon of the Colorado River on the boundary line between Arizona and Nevada. The power generated by the Hoover Dam goes to the people of southern California, Arizona, and Nevada. While the Niagara Falls, the TVA, and Hoover Dam are very impressive, there are 58,000 other hydroelectric plants in the United States.

For years, water and wind power have been neglected because oil was cheap and available. But, our energy needs are growing and our oil is running out. Many people want that limited oil for their cars, motorcycles, machines, and homes.

The demand for the limited supply of oil makes the price rise. Oil is getting very expensive. We are looking to other forms of energy to meet our needs. We are looking at wind and water for energy.

Black Star/John Running

HOW DO WIND AND WATER POWER WORK?

Like a toy pinwheel, the blades of a windmill turn when the wind pushes against them. A shaft connected to the turning blades is made to turn also. The turning shaft can be connected to make a pump go up and down. When the wind blows, the pump will pump water.

Although it takes more power than a pump needs, this turning can also make a generator spin. A generator is a machine that changes mechanical energy into electrical energy. A generator on a windmill turns the wind power into electrical power.

Electrical power from the wind was first used by farmers who wanted to listen to their favorite shows on the radio. The radio was hooked up to the electricity traveling down a wire from the windmill generator.

Generators can also send their current flowing along wires to be used kilometers away from where it is generated. For example, most electrical power companies run a number of generating stations at various locations. The lines that carry the current from one station are usually connected in a network with the lines from their other stations. If one station receives a demand for more electricity than it is making, it can call on the other stations to help meet the demand.

This happens on a hot day when many people turn on their air conditioners. Local power companies look for power from other areas where there is extra.

This giant interconnecting network of electrical lines is called a national power grid.

Electricity is carried to various parts of the country along power lines (above).

A grid provides reserves of electrical power.

Generators can also charge batteries for times when the wind doesn't blow. Many batteries are needed to store enough electricity. Since storing electricity in batteries takes up so much room, it must be stored in other ways, too.

Electricity can be made to charge up water to make hydrogen. Each molecule of water is made up of two atoms of hydrogen and one atom of oxygen. Hydrogen is a gas that is odorless and colorless. It can be burned for heat in much the same way that you could burn wood. Hydrogen can be carried on trucks. It can also be stored up and burned to make steam to turn turbines that make electricity on calm days.

Water rushing over water wheels can turn giant grinding stones called millstones. These make grain into flour. Some of

Generating stations send electric current along networks of power lines such as those at the right.

This Renaissance watermill utilized an undershot wheel to grind grain into flour.

these wheels are mounted in a river and just turn gently with the flow of the river. This kind of water wheel is called an undershot wheel. The undershot wheel is the most basic of water wheels. It was used as early as 100 B.C.

A more complicated water wheel uses water that is directed from the river into a chute. A wheel is mounted under the chute. The wheel has many scooplike buckets around its edge. The water flows out the chute to the top of the wheel. This kind of wheel is called an overshot wheel. The weight of the water falling into the buckets causes the wheel to turn. The turning of the wheel could be quickened or slowed by controlling the amount of water coming out of the chute. When the wheel turns, an axle or shaft turns. The turning axle could be connected by belts or gears to machinery inside a building.

Once inside, the power could be used to turn giant millstones. Or, the axle could turn gears and belts that move a sawblade that cuts trees up into boards. The power of the rushing water is used directly to operate machines.

The power of rushing water can also be harnessed by dams to make electricity. Dams hold back a river's water. When a dam is opened up, it makes a waterfall. The waterfall rushing over the dam hits blades of huge and complicated wheels called turbines. The rushing water causes them to turn around at tremendous speeds. The moving turbine turns a generator. The generator turns water power into electrical power.

The greater the force of the water, the faster the turbine will spin the generator. This is one way to use water power to make electricity. Electrical current can then be sent along wires and cables to people who need it.

Another way to make electricity from water is by using the heat in the water.

The sea is the world's largest solar collector. The temperature of the sea's surface is higher than the deep sea because it's collecting the heat of the sun that shines on it.

A century ago, Arsène d'Arsonval imagined a power generator which used the temperature difference in tropical waters to make electricity. Modern scientists

A modern dam.

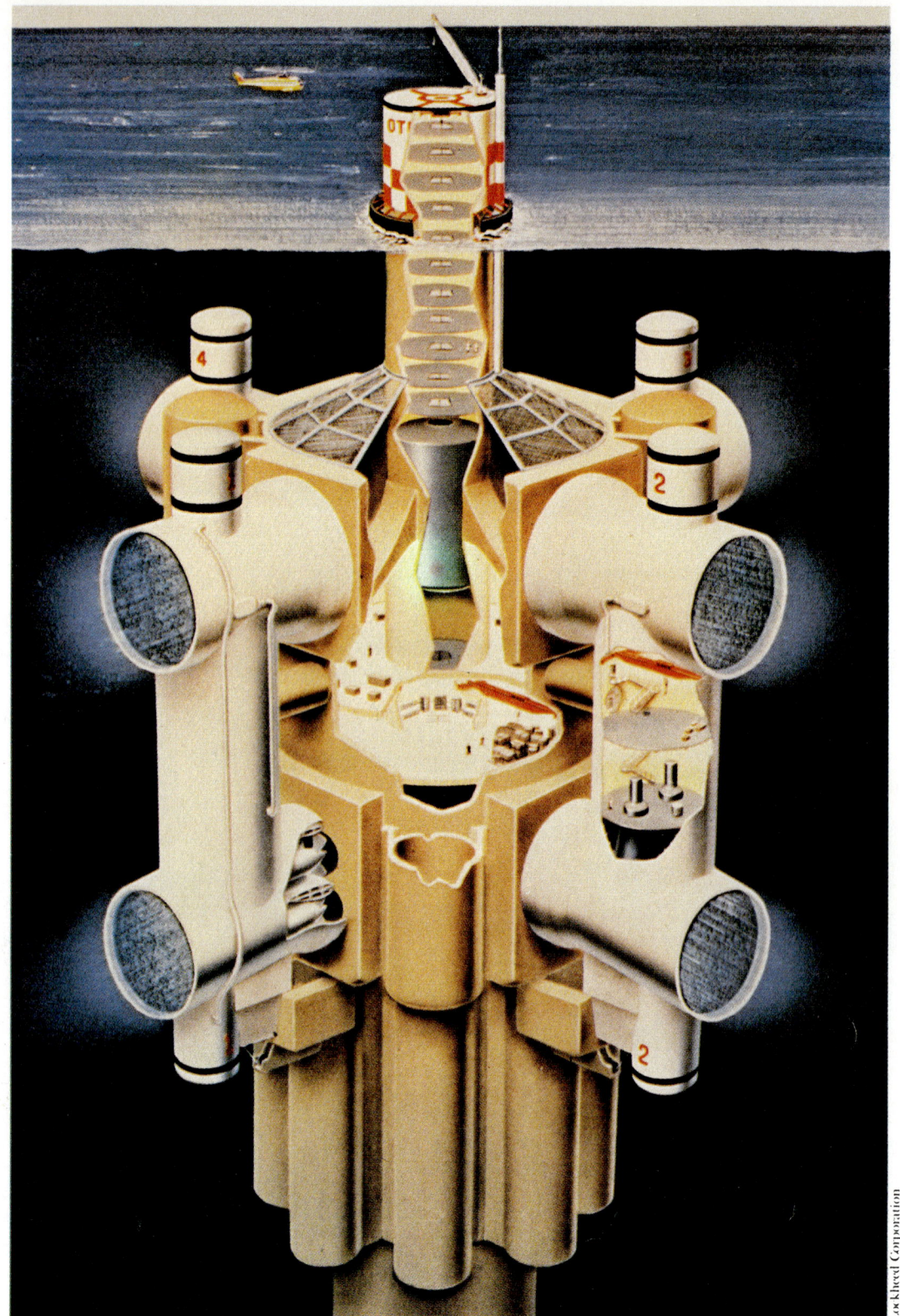

Lockheed Corporation

agree with d'Arsonval's idea. They have named this process Ocean Thermal Energy Conversion, or OTEC for short. Unlike a hydroelectric plant that uses the power from the rushing waterfall, the OTEC plant runs on heat from the ocean.

A fluid with a low boiling point, like propane or ammonia, can be boiled by the warm surface water. This boiling creates a gas that turns the blades of a turbine. The used gas is then cooled down by cold water pumped up from deep in the ocean. The cooling turns the gas back into a liquid. This is repeated again and again to run the turbine.

The turbine turns the generator to make electrical current. Electrical current could be used at the OTEC site for making some products which use large quantities of electricity. Or, electrical current could be sent to shore by well-insulated cables.

OTECs could be built on a large floating platform about the size of a football field. The pipe which brings the cold water from the ocean depths would be about 14 meters (45 ft) across and 600 to 900 meters (2,000 to 3,000 ft) long.

Several plants based on d'Arsonval's idea have been built. One, built in Cuba's Bay of Matazanzas in 1929 by a student of d'Arsonval, generated enough power to run the plant, but no more. Then waves and currents destroyed the iron cold-water pipe. In the early 1950s, another

The U.S. Navy tanker SS Ocean Thermal Converter *(below) was converted into an OTEC test platform to evaluate the OTEC concept.*

U.S. Department of Energy

At the left is a painting showing a cutaway view of an OTEC platform.

27

French group tried again off the Ivory Coast in Africa. That project also met with mechanical as well as political problems.

In 1980, a group of three companies and the state of Hawaii launched a mini-OTEC that generated 12 kilowatts. Now, the U.S. government is experimenting with an old Navy tanker refitted to be an energy lab. The SS *Ocean Energy Converter* will help future builders of OTECs avoid costly mistakes. A government agency called the Office of Ocean Minerals and Energy feels a plant generating 40 to 80 megawatts will be operating in U.S. waters by 1986 to 1988. They think it will probably be located off Hawaii or Guam.

There are good reasons for developing OTECs. They can generate power 24 hours a day, rain or shine. But they must be located in waters where the sun-warmed surface waters can boil their chemicals. For this reason, OTECs are limited to tropical waters.

One day over 100 years ago, a man named William Bell Elliot was out hunting grizzly bear. He came over a hill and was amazed by the sight of steam pouring from cracks along the steep canyon. Mr. Elliot thought he'd discovered the gates of hell.

What he had discovered was the world's largest geothermal center, The Geysers. It is located about 90 miles north of San Francisco in California.

Geothermal heat comes from inside the earth. Magma is rock that has been melted by intense heat within the earth. This magma deep underground sends its heat to other rocks and to water that has filtered down from the surface. When the water is heated, it moves back toward the surface along cracks in the rock. It can shoot out of the ground as a geyser, or as a dry steam fumarole. Or, heated water can get trapped under the surface by dense cap rock. This water can be tapped by drilling a well. The steam from these hot geysers or wells can be harnessed to spin

This is a geothermal well in the geyser area of northern California.

turbines. The Geysers in California produces electricity that is used for heating and air conditioning homes in the area.

Dry steam fumaroles, like those found at The Geysers, can be used directly to drive turbine generators. Fumaroles occur at only a few places in the world. In the United States, there are two sites, The Geysers and Yellowstone National Park. Dry steam sites are also located in Italy, Russia, and Japan.

Japan first used geothermal heat for generating electricity in 1924. The Japanese now tap extensive steam fields at Beppu for heating, health spas, and even for restaurant cooking.

Hot springs can also provide energy. In Boise, Idaho, many homes are hooked up to hot spring water for heat in winter.

In California, developers plan a geothermal community where 4,000 homes would be heated by hot springs.

In addition to space heating, this hot but less than boiling water can be used to heat low boiling point liquids such as Freon and Isobutane. When these substances reach their boiling point, the resulting steam can drive turbine generators.

This is a cutaway drawing of the earth showing the source of geothermal energy.

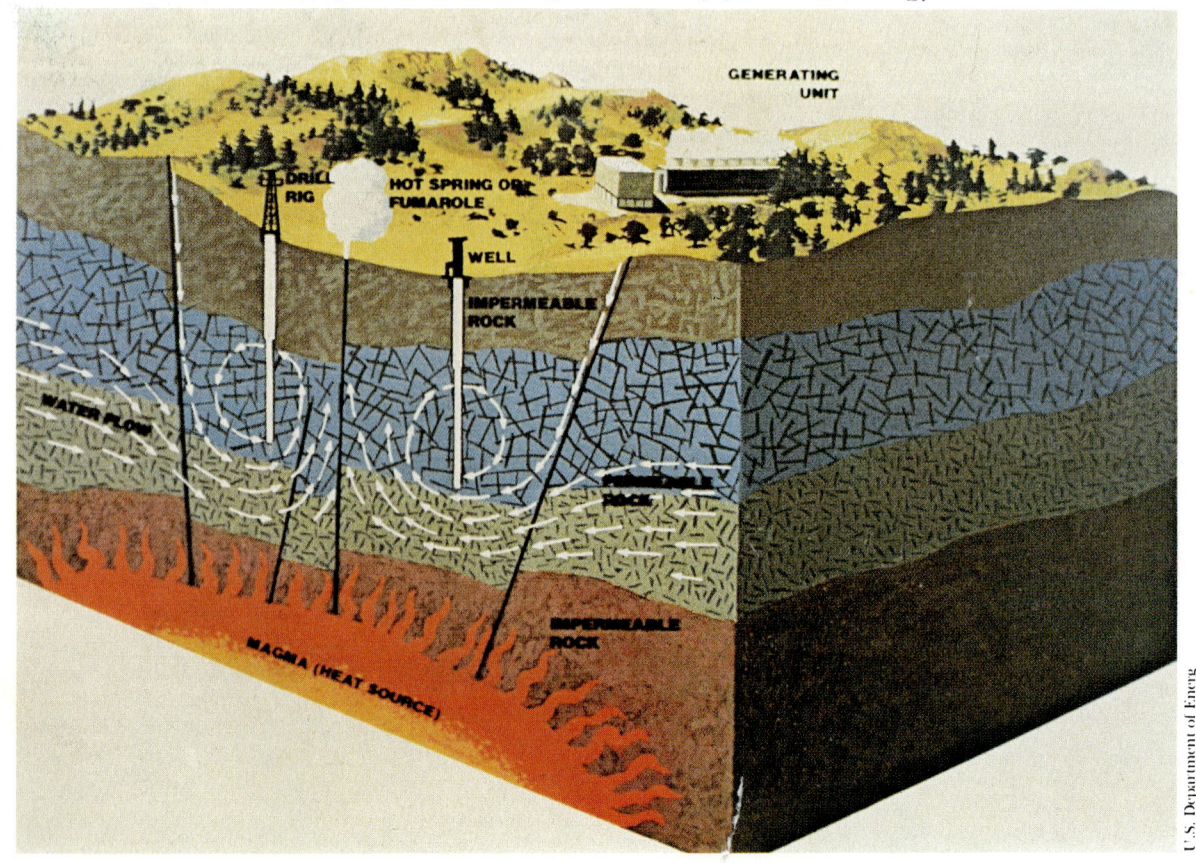

This technique is used on the Soviet peninsula of Kamchatka in the northwest Pacific Ocean. Also, geothermally heated water, less than boiling, can be used in many industrial processes such as drying hay.

All the buildings in Reykjavik, Iceland are heated by geothermal water. Many homes and commercial buildings are built right over hot spring water which is generally about 100°C (212°F). Several years ago, a family got more hydrothermal heat than they wanted when a crack opened in their kitchen floor and scalding water gushed into the house. This kind of accident is rare, however. Since no coal or oil is burned, the 115,000 people who live in Reykjavik enjoy one of the cleanest cities in the world.

This is a geothermal steam pipe at a power plant in northern California.

PRESENT AND FUTURE

The success of wind and water power depends on geography. A windmill built where only gentle breezes blow will not work. Wind energy is most practical for coastal regions and the Great Plains where the wind blows hardest.

Old-fashioned windmills were made out of cloth like sailboat sails. Some new designs for wind machines look like giant copies of kitchen tools. One design, the Darrieus Rotor, looks like a giant upright egg beater. Another looks like a giant spatula spinning around and around.

One design looks like a huge pinwheel. Another, the SST Wind Turbine, looks like a monster bicycle wheel with blades that snap into the spokes and respond quickly to changes in the wind.

Perhaps you have seen the windmill design that the National Aeronautics and Space Administration (NASA) is experimenting with. It looks like an airplane propeller. Each blade is 30

In a 13 kilometer-per-hour (8 mph) wind, this wind turbine can produce enough electricity to be used by 50 average homes.

meters (100 ft) long. High atop Howard Knob, near Boone, North Carolina, sits a two-megawatt NASA wind turbine. It started feeding electricity into the local power grid in 1979. The turbine is expected to provide enough electricity to supply about 300 to 500 average size homes at a wind speed of 40 kph (25 mph). Other NASA type wind machines are being tested near Sandusky, Ohio, with support from the U.S. Energy Research and Development Administration. Results of the tests may be applied to the development of larger wind-powered electrical sites.

One small windmill can provide enough energy for one family. Scientists picture wind farms of many acres of windmills in rows, which might make energy for nearby cities. In fact, Pacific Gas and Electric Company in San Francisco has signed a 30-year contract with a wind farm company to buy 35,000 kilowatts of power. Twenty-one wind machines 61 meters (200 ft) tall with 91 meter (300 ft) wide blades are scheduled to be built east of San Francisco. These machines are expected to make enough power to supply 150,000 homes.

Windmills can be used on offshore drilling rigs. They can supply the power to search for more oil.

Windmills are not the only machines that use the wind. Modern mechanical sails on oil tankers can save one-half of the power necessary to move a ship.

Blimps filled with special gases may soon ride the wind currents to move cargo. This could be cheaper than airplanes. A giant lighter-than-air craft is nearing completion at the Lakehurst Naval Air Engineering Center and will be tested soon. Helium-filled blimps have shown that they are economical for heavy lifting. Their ability to lift up to

This Japanese tanker uses special sails, which cut in half the amount of fuel it burns.

24 tons will make them good movers for oil derricks and pipelines and military equipment. Can you imagine an army tank floating gently along in the breeze?

Water power depends on local geography, too. We know that an OTEC needs tropical waters. There are other locations in the ocean that can generate power.

The Gulf Stream is like a giant river that runs in the Atlantic Ocean. It flows from Cuba up the coast of North America. From there, it crosses the ocean to empty into the Arctic Sea. It has a flow five times greater than all the water in all the rivers of the world.

This speedy underwater current may someday turn huge water wheels that will spin turbines and produce electricity. Undersea windmills may someday produce lots of electricity for the people of Florida.

Have you ever seen a piece of wood tossed about by the force of the waves in a lake or ocean? On the coast of Oregon, waves threw a rock that weighed about as much as a grown woman through the roof of a lighthouse. The lighthouse was on a cliff 41 meters (135 ft) above the water!

The waves that crash against northern Hawaii are often 30 to 60 meters (100 to 200 ft) high. Waters around the British Isles are wild with waves, too.

Wave power can be harnessed. A floating power station as large as an oil tanker could be

Jack Jackso

Floating power stations may some day harness the power of waves.

36

anchored in the waves. Lopsided metal vanes inside would rock up and down with the passing waves. The wave power would turn generators to make electricity. Cables would carry the electricity to shore.

The British Government is very interested in wave power. It has begun experimenting with floating generators off Scotland's coast.

The power of the tides can generate electricity, too. If we could harness the energy of tides, there would be enough energy to supply many of our needs. We could do this by making the rising and falling water flow through turbines to make electricity. However, this would require tremendous construction of dams and turbines. Only a few places in the world have enough rise and fall of the tides to make this expensive construction worthwhile.

A large tidal power station is located in the English Channel off the coast of France. The tides produce 240 megawatts of electricity a day. That's about as much power as a a small nuclear plant produces. A smaller tidal power station is located on the Barents Sea in Russia.

Canada has the biggest tidal rise and fall in the whole world. It measures nearly 17 meters (55 ft) on the Bay of Fundy in Nova Scotia. Every 12 hours more than 2 billion tons of water surge in and out.

For several years, hundreds of people worked to build dams and build the generators to harness the power of the tide. But the strength of the tide they tried to tame made work very slow and difficult. Finally, the Bay of Fundy Project was scrapped because it was just too expensive. As the price of oil continues to rise, however, this project may again be attempted. Harnessing this tidal power is still the dream of scientists. They are studying the possibility of a series of dams to capture the power from the strong tide.

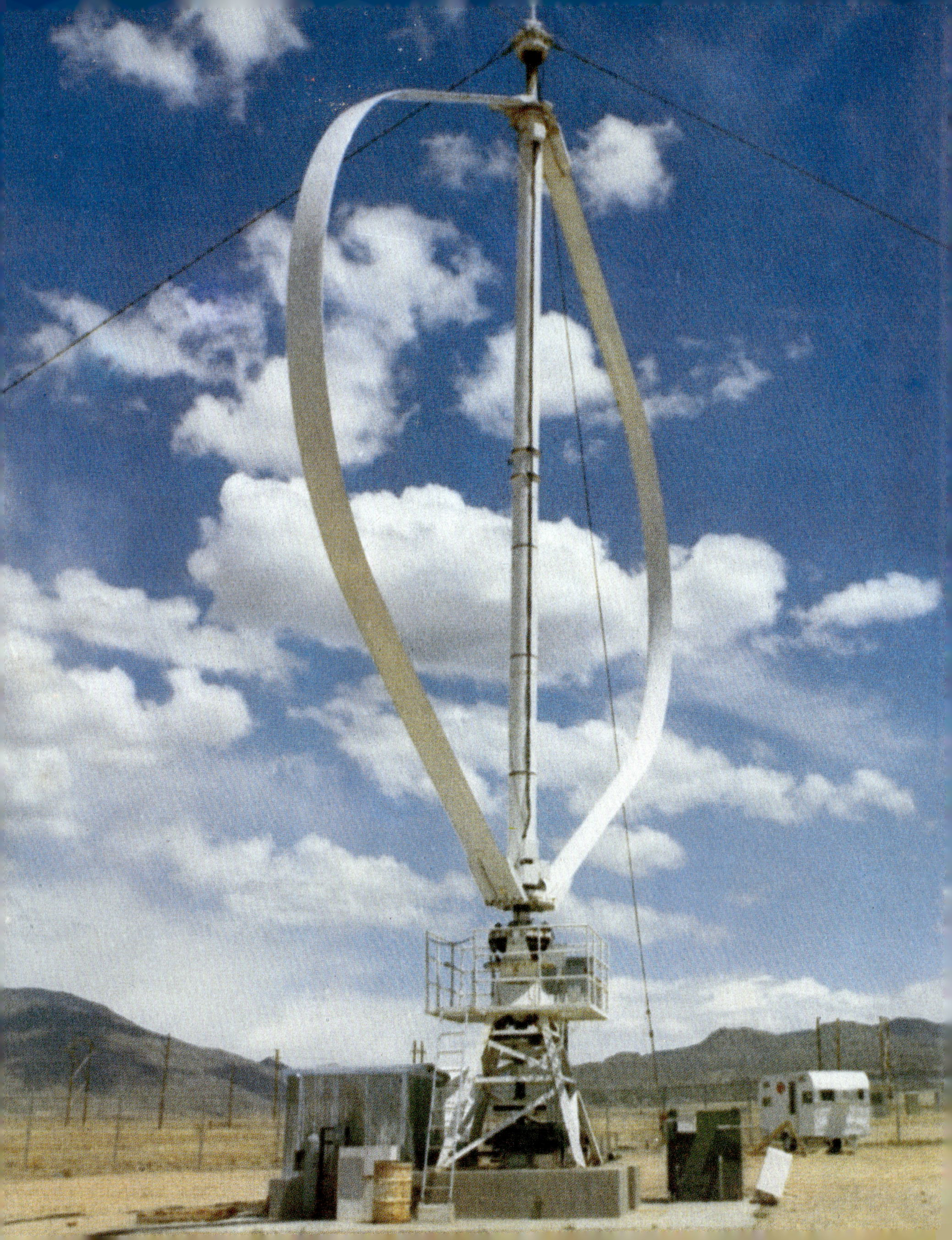

SOLUTIONS AND PROBLEMS

Wind and water are free, but machines to harness their power are not. Expensive machinery is just one problem. As the price of oil continues to climb, however, alternate energy producers will be able to compete.

Small windmills on farms cause no problems. But, if windmills are used to generate power for cities, they might be very large. Or, they might be built close to cities. Would you mind living near a windmill? Some people think wind machines are ugly to look at. We must make sure windmills are placed so that they do not cause visual pollution.

Many windmills located together on wind farms will need a lot of land. Farmers might want to use the same land to grow food. Land use must be planned so that there is enough land for both windmills and farmers.

If many windmills are located together, migrating birds could crash into them. We must study the paths birds take when they

This is a vertical axis wind turbine (VAWT). Its blades provide power regardless of the wind direction.

migrate. Then windmills can be built out of the birds' way.

The biggest problem with wind power is that the wind doesn't always blow. Energy must be stored up for calm days. Storage batteries take up a lot of space.

If electricity made by the wind is passed through water, hydrogen gas is released from the water. Hydrogen can be stored, and sent to where it is needed. Hydrogen gas, like the natural gas that is burned by some of our furnaces, is burned to heat water to make steam. The steam then can turn the electrical generators when there is no wind. Hydrogen can be combined with rotting grass or other organic matter to make fuels such as methane which can power cars.

A major problem with hydrogen is that it can explode. Even so, some scientists feel that the storage problem of wind power will be solved by using hydrogen.

Water power also poses some problems. Water passing over dams makes a lot of electricity. But, if a dam collapses, the rushing waters could bury the cities and towns downstream. Dam failures are rare, but must be considered. The Army Corps of Engineers is responsible for inspecting dams to make sure they are safe.

Another problem with building dams is that they take up a lot of land and change the way the water flows. The Tellico Dam in Tennessee is a recent example. Many people were concerned that building this dam would forever destroy a tiny fish called the snail darter. It was believed that this was the only place in the world it existed. Now, however, it has been discovered elsewhere. Do we, in our desire for more power, have the right to cause a creature's extinction?

Another problem with the Tellico Dam is that people would be moved off their land so the reservoir could be built. The people who live there are farmers. They are farming the same land that their grandfathers farmed. They like their farms.

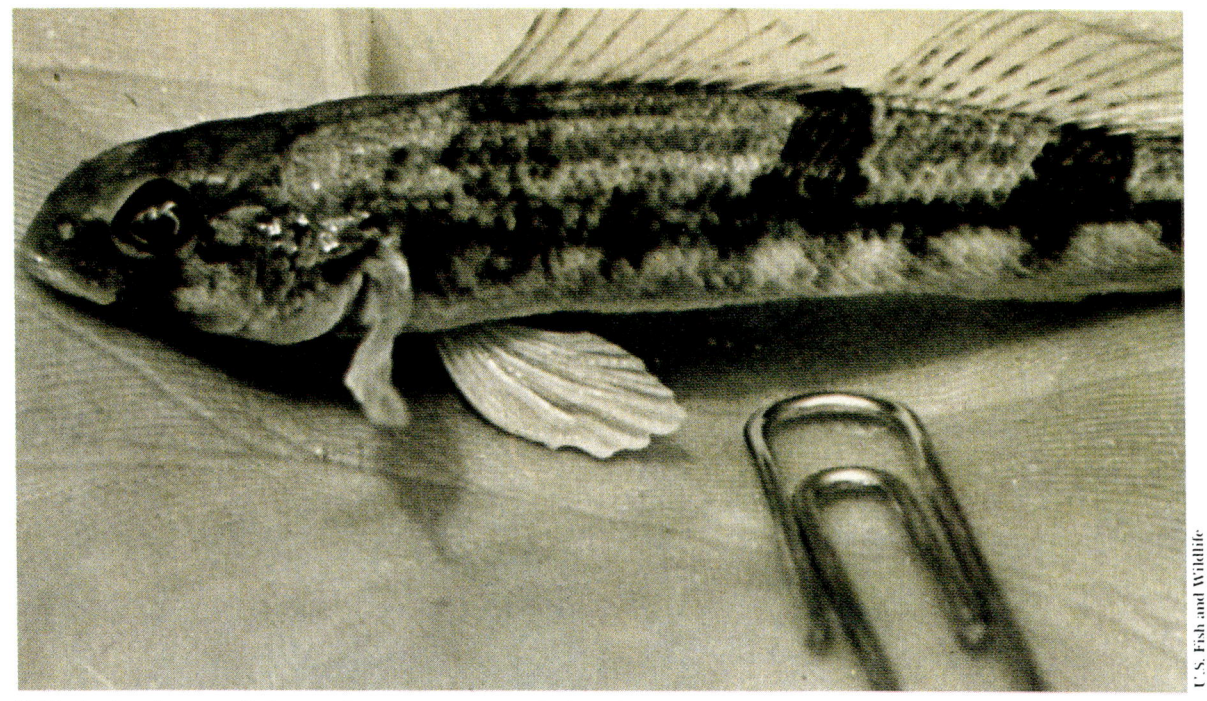

This is the tiny snail darter. It was once feared that the building of a dam would kill all these fish.

They don't want to move. Balancing an individual's rights against our energy needs is a sticky job.

OTECs and machinery to harness wave, current, and tidal power must share the seas with ships. Ship operators are afraid they might crash into these power stations. These stations will have to be well marked. Shippers will have to be kept informed of the locations of the power stations.

Many kinds of fish and marine life must also share the seas. Leaking chemicals from machinery in the water could kill some marine life. Constant inspections are vital.

OTECs pump up large amounts of cold water from the ocean depths. When plants and animals that live in the ocean die, their remains sink to the bottom.

So, the cold lower waters are rich in nutrients. Pumping up this water would disturb the natural life cycles of marine life. This balance must be studied and understood.

Tidal projects must be careful not to interfere with the migration patterns of the creatures that live in the sea.

And, a project that uses water wheels to trap the power of the Gulf Stream must keep track of all side effects such as the cooling or slowing of the Gulf Stream. Such a cooling or slowing could alter the weather on the other side of the ocean.

On land, geothermal sites generate much electricity. But, as steam and water hiss or bubble from the ground, minerals and other dissolved substances come along. Sulfur is one substance that comes up with the steam. Sulfur smells like rotten eggs. Sailors can smell the coast of Iceland before they can see it through the mist. We all want enough power for our radios and TVs, but do we want to live near noisy, smelly geothermal sites? Also, as the geothermally heated water is removed from the ground, no one knows what will happen. The earth could cave in. Used water must be pumped back into the ground.

Another problem is that research and development of these new methods of generating power costs a lot of money before the new methods make one watt of power. Many people think that their taxes are too high already. They don't want the government to spend money on new projects. So, because they will run out of money, some test projects will just have to shut down.

Water and wind power make no radioactive waste. Water and wind power cause no strip mining scars. Water and wind power will last as long as the earth lasts. But we must act responsibly as we harness the waters and winds.

42

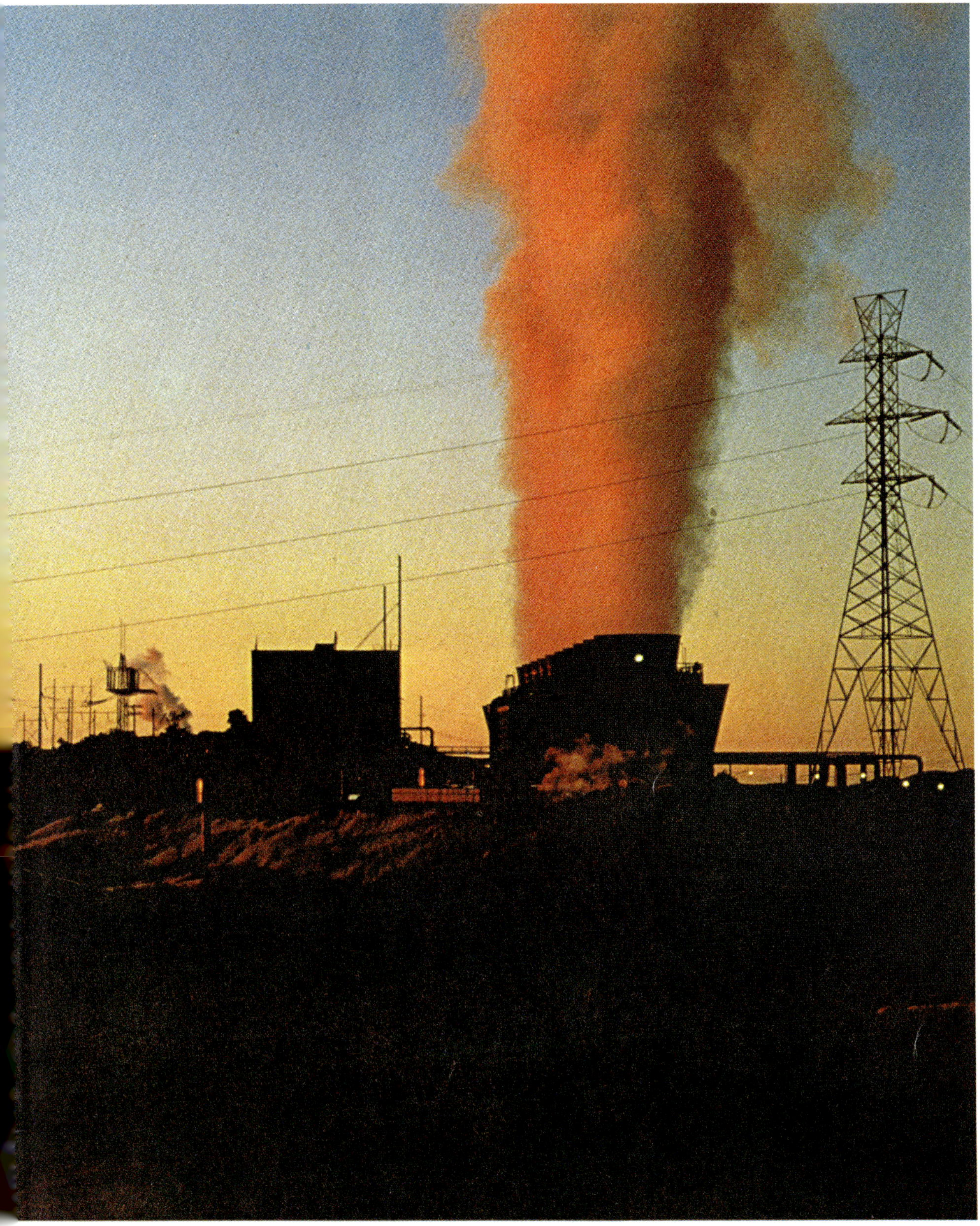

MAKE YOUR OWN WATER WHEEL

You can make a waterwheel just like the ones that have been used for centuries in mills. You'll probably want an adult to help you with the hammering, and cutting the Ping-Pong balls.

Materials

1 piece of 1 inch plywood, cut in a circle about 20 inches wide (can be adjusted for your sink)
7 Ping-Pong balls cut in half
Epoxy glue
1 ¼ inch metal rod
2 pieces of board, about 1 inch wide, and a little longer than the sink
2 long nails
1 hammer
(Optional: a bicycle generator)

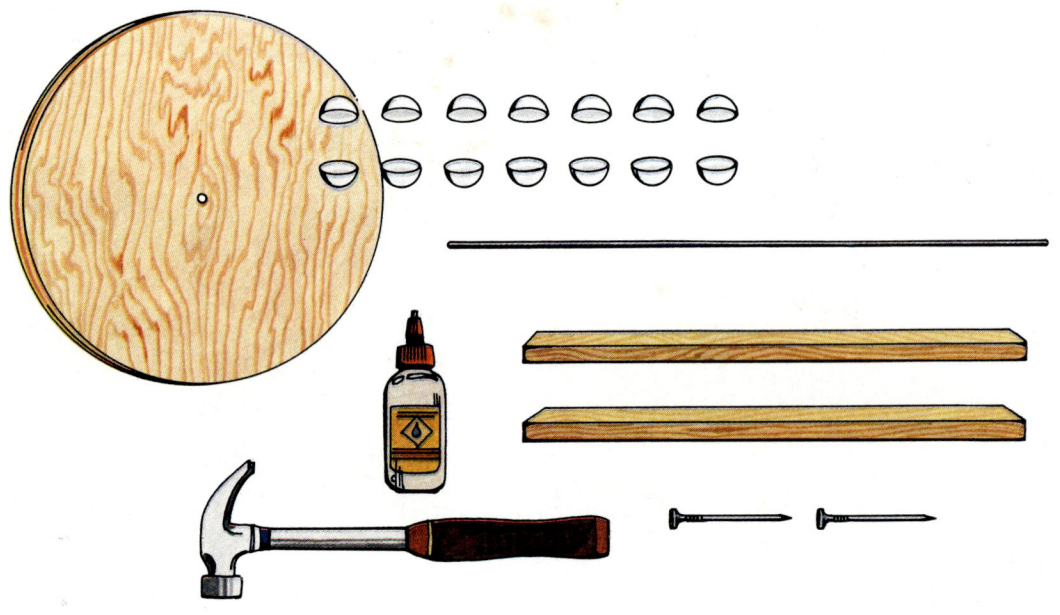

Jerry Scott

44

1. Make a ⅛ inch hole in the center of the wooden circle. Make sure you have a tight enough fit to turn the wheel.
2. Glue the balls with epoxy to the rim of the wheel. Space them evenly. 
3. Push the rod through the hole. If the rod is loose, push some epoxy into the hole to hold it firmly.
4. Carefully hammer one nail about ½ inch down into each board. 
5. Rest the ends of the rod on the boards, right next to the nails. Gently hammer the sides of the nails until they bend over and touch the board on the other side of the rod. Make sure you leave room for the rod to turn.
6. Set up your waterwheel so that it is directly under the water from the faucet. Turn the water on so it hits the cups on the wheel. The wheel will spin around.

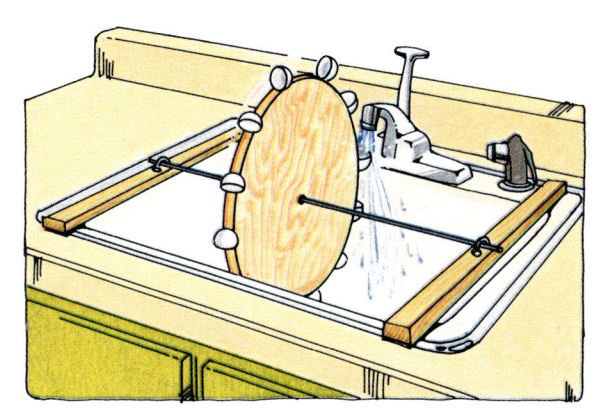

Note: If you have a small generator, like a bicycle generator, you could try hooking it up to the turning rod. It would have to be held very firmly near the sink. You could attach it to the rod with a thick rubber band.

45

PRONUNCIATION GUIDE

These symbols have the same sound as the darker letters in the sample words.

ə	b**a**lloon, ag**o**
a	m**a**p, h**a**ve
ä	f**a**ther, c**a**r
b	**b**all, ri**b**
d	**d**id, a**dd**
e	b**e**ll, g**e**t
ē	k**ee**n, l**ea**p
f	**f**an, so**f**t
g	**g**ood, bi**g**
h	**h**urt, a**h**ead
i	r**i**p, **i**ll
ī	s**i**de, sk**y**
j	**j**oin, **g**erm
k	**k**ing, as**k**
l	**l**et, coo**l**
m	**m**an, sa**m**e
n	**n**o, tur**n**
ō	c**o**ne, kn**ow**
ȯ	**a**ll, s**aw**
p	**p**art, scra**p**
r	**r**oot, ti**r**e
s	**s**o, pre**ss**
sh	**sh**oot, ma**ch**ine
t	**t**o, s**t**and
ü	p**oo**l, l**o**se
u̇	p**u**t, b**oo**k
v	**v**iew, gi**v**e
w	**w**ood, glo**w**ing
y	**y**es, **y**ear
′	accent

GLOSSARY

These words are defined the way they are used in the book.

current (kər′ ənt) water that flows steadily in one direction

fumarole (fyü′ mə rōl) a hole in volcanic ground through which hot vapors escape

generator (jen′ ə rāt ər) a machine that changes mechanical energy, such as a spinning wheel, into electrical energy

geothermal (jē ō thər′ məl) having to do with heat from inside the earth

geyser (gī′ zər) hot water and steam that shoots up from cracks in the ground

hydroelectric (hī drō i lek′ trik) having to do with the production of electricity from water

magma (mag′ mə) hot, melted rock within the earth

megawatt (meg′ ə wät) one million watts; a watt is the standard unit of power

overshot (ō′ vər shät) being moved by water falling from above

thermal (thər′ məl) having to do with heat

turbine (tər′ bən) an engine that is powered by spinning blades

undershot (ən′ dər shät) being moved by water passing underneath

INDEX

blimp, 34-36
coal, 31
current (water), 6, 17, 41
dam, 17-18, 24, 37, 40-41
dike, 11
electricity, 6, 7, 12, 13, 17, 18, 21, 22, 24-25, 27, 29, 30, 34, 36, 37, 40
Franklin, Benjamin, 17
fumarole, 8, 28, 29-30
generator, 6, 21, 22, 24-25, 27, 29, 37, 40
geothermal energy, 7,
geothermal heat, 28, 30, 31
geyser, 7-8, 28
Geysers, The, 8, 28, 29
Gulf Stream, 17, 36, 42
Hoover Dam, 18
hot spring, 7, 8, 30, 31
hydroelectric power, 6
hydroelectric power plant, 18
hydrogen, 22, 40
magma, 28
National Aeronautics and Space Administration (NASA), 33-34
national power grid, 22
Ocean Thermal Energy Conversion (OTEC), 27, 28, 36, 41
oil, 12-13, 14, 18, 31, 34, 37, 39
Old Faithful, 8
overshot wheel, 24
power grid, 34
power station, 12

Rural Electrification Administration, 12
Smith-Putnam Wind Turbine, 13-14
solar energy, 5
sulfur, 42
Tennessee Valley Authority (TVA), 18
tidal power, 37, 41
tidal power station, 37
tide, 6, 14-15, 37
turbine, 22, 24-25, 27, 29, 30, 36, 37
undershot wheel, 24
water, 22
water power, 5-6, 14, 17-18, 24-25, 33, 36, 40, 42
water wheel, 6, 22-24, 36, 42
wave, 6,
wave power, 36-37, 41
wind, 5
wind farm, 34, 39-40
windmill, 11, 12, 13, 21, 33, 34, 36, 39-40
wind power, 11, 18, 21, 33, 40, 42
wind turbine, 33, 34

C.2

333.91
P   Payne, Sherry Neu-
            wirth

         Wind and water
         energy

DATE DUE

ASHFORD ELEMENTARY SCHOOL